WHAT LIGHT
HE SAW
I CANNOT
SAY

Southern Messenger Poets

DAVE SMITH, SERIES EDITOR

WHAT LIGHT
HE SAW
I CANNOT
SAY

poems

Sidney Burris

LOUISIANA STATE UNIVERSITY PRESS   BATON ROUGE

Published by Louisiana State University Press
www.lsupress.org

LSU Press Paperback Original

DESIGNER: Michelle A. Neustrom
TYPEFACE: Cochin, display; Whitman, text

Grateful acknowledgment is extended to the following journals
in which some of these poems originally appeared:

American Journal of Poetry: "Poem for High Summer," "Drinking Nettle Tea,
Reading Milarepa," and "American City, Broken Body"; *Blackbird: An Online Journal
of Literature and the Arts*: "Aubade: Homesong" and "Dream Cargo"; *The Harvard
Review*: "Nocturne: Pascal Says"; *IthacaLit*: "Slag Watch" and "Transfiguration:
Gray Sky Good Enough to Wear"; and *Third Wednesday*: "The True
Subject: Self-Portrait with Dogwood."

COVER IMAGE: MRaust/iStock.com

LIBRARY OF CONGRESS CATALOGING-IN-PUBLICATION DATA

Names: Burris, Sidney, 1953– author.
Title: What light he saw I cannot say : poems / Sidney Burris.
Description: Baton Rouge : Louisiana State University Press, [2021] | Series: Southern
  messenger poets
Identifiers: LCCN 2020032850 (print) | LCCN 2020032851 (ebook) | ISBN 978-0-8071-7336-7
  (paperback) | ISBN 978-0-8071-7521-7 (pdf) | ISBN 978-0-8071-7522-4 (epub)
Subjects: LCGFT: Poetry.
Classification: LCC PS3552.U7437 W48 2021 (print) | LCC PS3552.U7437 (ebook) | DDC
  811/.54—dc23
LC record available at https://lccn.loc.gov/2020032850
LC ebook record available at https://lccn.loc.gov/2020032851

For the three lights I *have* seen and will always love:
Angie, Elizabeth, and Sam

CONTENTS

III

IV

I

RUNOFF

January's drop-down menu
leaves everything to the imagination:
splotch the ice, splice the light,
remake the spirit . . .

Just get on with it,
doing what you have to do
with the gray palette that lies
to hand. The sun's coming soon.

A future, then, of warmth and runoff,
and old faces surprised to see us.
A cache of love, I'd call it,
opened up, vernal, refreshed.

RIGGING AND STEERAGE

Late winter, the cold buckles and drops its rigging and steerage:
leaves cloistered in the amber corner of my yard everlasting,
the bagworm's lace still hung in the hickory.
                                        Nothing here
in this moment lies beyond the hazy path of passage . . .

But what a moment it is, unfrozen, on the move, as it was in the beginning,
long before I saw it, a confetti leaf-fall from God knows where,
slashed across the yard, at wind-cut angles I couldn't measure in this mess.

And so am standing here, going nowhere in the immeasurable geometry
of evening and sunset and dusk,
all of which come early to those who grieve
but are not haunted and are aware.

THE WORLD IS MOVING ON,
AND I HAVE MORE TO SAY

Here's a way for me to say
I'm sorry you suffered hard things
once when I wasn't around.
Still, these hard things, they rain down and rain down,
and still a line or two is all I've got to throw across the gulf between us.

We can talk about praying they stop, these choking dreams,
about how you know things I don't, have things to do
I won't, how these monsoons of grief
and rage come and go . . .

But now I see you leaving for the day
as March muscles its way through the maple.
The world's always moving I once read, but not now,
please not now, I have so much more to say.

STILL LIFE WITH HAWK

1.

To explain what happened, to get to the bottom of it,
       between shade, shadow, mote, and sun,
            a single set of words where I'd live and work,
a place undone by nothing . . .

2.

I think of fence lines and frost-light.
       Virginia. Cold air. Glassy pastures, not yet broken.
        One hawk, sentry to the stillness everywhere.
Then comes a boy. Then a boy's heart. Both, astonished to be there.

3.

To hold this in a poem,
       to take the world as it is, or was,
         riding power lines that dip and rise,
along this blacktop, up that hill, and down the other side,

4.

telling anyone who'd dare listen
       about the flashes and specks and blades of grass
         that make a day . . . to hold
all of this in a poem . . . that was once the dream, but no more.

5.

Confession: now, the strangeness of the greening world,
       the sun's long pull across the sky,
         these should be enough, all I need to get by,
and yet, most times, they're not. So, again: I've thinly known myself.

6.

When I am sad, said my old heart last night, *the trees darken,*
    the upstart air lumbers along with grief.
        I have thought about this over and over, alert as a hawk,
and now have seen it: the heart's a dark, lumbering place.

7.

Whatever rustles in the rustling world will one day rise and fly away.
    I know this to be true as well.
        See? says my old heart. *The lumbering loblollies*
    rustled once
and shook their grief away . . . My old joyous heart! Won't you come
    and stay?

8.

No, not yet, there's so much work left to do.
    I see the coming, the going, but not the speed of it all,
        a friend lost, a goldfinch on the feeder,
the wind parsed into prayers I hear slipping through the eaves.

9.

It's true, too, about the holy ones, they're on their knees under
    unruly skies.
    The singers are at their songs, the ships hard on their seas.
        I have nothing so grand in mind. A few words here,
    a few there,
short solos in tune with a cold afternoon's hum and drill, at ease

10.

with the hard end of a looping winter. I'll crackle as I can,
    and then I'm done, boots on, flat out in high cotton
        that runs all the way to the blue sky:
a way of being in a place that's all about light-slant, shadow-play,

11.

constant motion. In short: how to be in a place that's never been
     the way it seemed to be. That's the trick. So maybe lay me
     down faceup,
         with a good view of Arcturus, maybe trust the ellipses
     in our lives,
hawk and talon, the air the day you noticed something odd, and let me
     go at that.

LAMENTATION, DOMINION, EXTINCTION

The laggard moon's out of its lair.
Evening slinks in, softening the yard's stark lines . . .
Definition's replaced now by suggestion,
                          and the willow over there suggests
lamentation.
Its moon-wet limbs are wailing without a sound.

I don't know how that happened,
how the willow got inside me,
but I've taken to heart its lash and burn,
                          I've huddled under its smoky
dominion
for so long, I swore it was my birthright, this huddling.

So I'm searching out these endings all around me now,
these little elegies lying everywhere,
like the Nightshade in full flower under the willow,
                          and how it skirts
extinction.
I can do this too, revenant, out of the shadows to prowl, to thrive,
        to bloom.

DREAM CARGO

1.

Mid-morning, midlife, freighted
        still from a night's dreaming,
sunrise done, pageant gone,
        careening now toward noon and glare,
disheveled and defiled . . .
        a good time to say what lies ahead:
after dustfall and the body's decrescendo,
        after the maple's first gleam goes flat,
there's a burnish to autumn
        you learn to live for: oblivion's
pocket runs deep in our lives,
        the charnel crows fly overhead.

2.

Maybe it's Troy we ought to think of here,
        and the blood-cost of beauty,
the old destiny of passion and war,
        and the windowless eyes of the ravaged.

3.

Ever notice how slip-shod smoke is,
        drifting, homeless, how it just curls and vanishes?
So now think of souls in flight,
        smoke-drift, migration, a flock
of two, you and me down the road.
        Lord, how we proliferate
and fade away; Lord, how piecemeal we die.

4.

This is nowhere near the whole truth.

    There's another kind of dying we survive
to become a carapace,

    a reliquary,
and one you know all too well: I saw it,

5. Leda

your eye's fear-flash, felt the weight

    of the air and crush of wings
everywhere as you told me

    your ancient story and how it
plunders you still and drops you dawn-

    cold in bed, night in and night out.
You did not dream this story,

    though like a dream, it lingers
long after it found you, this ravaging

    from that famous old Greek myth.

6.

And still the truck in my dream rolled on down

    the road, hauling its dream cargo,
you and me, side by side, heather

    and gorse, blossom and bruise on the lam.

7.

Could it be dreaming's all that's left of prayer?

    May our dreams then proliferate,
and drift away where we cannot

    get at them, and savage them.
May they drift upward without us,

    you and I, soul's husks, hunkered down
here on this blue orphan earth, for better

    or worse, our sapphire in the star-field.

TOWARD THE MIDDLE OF THE NIGHT,
I HEAR THE QUESTION,
HOW WILL YOU SPEND YOUR DAYS?

for my daughter, Elizabeth

Only in song, only in praise, I say,
    the phrase I'm taught by the better spirits
        that lay in wait as yard-light declines

then curls upward, fireflies
    in my daughter's hands,
        the gold sifting through her fingers like sand.

And so these spirits, no more than memorable light, really,
    come and find us deep in the night,
        and say, sing, man, and praise, child . . .

because you alone can raise the dead
    as the dead have raised you,
        and so we do, my daughter and I,

under moon and sun thatched
    in the moment when both are clear
        on their horizons and working hard the light

they have to give. It's said the wise laugh only
    with fear and trembling,
        but we can't help ourselves,

or won't, and are bent over double
    and can't remember, even if you'd ask,
        what brought us here, and why we laugh.

TWO STATEMENTS BY PASCAL

I guess the bleached shoreline of late afternoon
is a border of some sort,
                              and I don't know why I bother
with imagined provinces, or the invocation of breakdown,
boogie-woogie word-hoards,
or why I've come to love the migration of birds . . .

All the things I love I've learned to love in passing.

But I do know that in times of crossing
                              and wind-shift,
whatever's left unsaid is usually left for dead: a blessed crosswind arrives,
and I'm off the straight and narrow
                              and into cloistered alcoves
that echo with thrush-song and psalm,
                              and here I know I'm home . . .

It's 1960, a Virginia mill town,
                              my seventh year to Heaven,
and Father McClintock, Anglican, having drifted south from MIT
with his raven cassock and austere theology,

                                        stoops
to enter the sacristy,
                    returns
downloaded with gravity and grace, a candle in one hand,
a chalice in the other, and lumbers down the hall, out of sight.
His darkness was years in the making, they said,
                              but when it descended for good,
he took to his bed and shook like a piece of foil
                              until he could shake no more.
Then died in darkness.

A Mardi Gras of shadows
parades into our yards,
leaning against our houses, year by year, until we let them in.

Pascal claimed that thinking too little about things,

                                or too much,

makes us obstinate and fanatical.

Obstinate and fanatical,
I have grown to know this place where I live.
It is the low tide of late afternoon.
Starlings have mustered their consolation.

Pascal also said that to live by one's work alone,

                            and to reign

over the most powerful state in the world are two very different things,
a helpful midlife correction.
My Shrove willow sheds its leaves, and litters the kingdom
of my yard, its work for the year done, and done well.
Across the sky, a comet hauls its light and writes its life:
we spark and fade, I learn, and are born to trouble.

I have thought a great deal about this,
and not at all.

Either way, though, we spark and fade.
Either way, we wander about in times that do not belong to us.
Either way, we spark
and fade.

ANNUAL REPORT

2.15.2017

What I like about everything
        is nothing's ever finished.
This poem, for example,
        an order of words,

set down with intention
        and purpose, known
only to the few
        who happen on it,

like those winter bulbs
        my daughter planted and forgot
until one day down fell the sunlight,
        up rose the jonquil

and the evening,
        after all was said and done,
looked to both of us to be
        just about right.

4.12.2017

Besides, I'd really prefer joy ride the air of this hard year
        so I could breathe it in at will,
but nothing ever happens that way and wishing won't make it so
        even though the air ripples, the clouds gang up
in evening pink, and I've cast my questions across the universe
        and stand here, heronlike, watching the shallows
for the tell-tale flash I once took for an answer.
        I won't dress up what I've discovered:
there's no ladder to the stars, no highway to Hell, no way of saying
        what happened without the blue remorse
of knowing I could've said it another way, as I stand here knee-deep,

still in the shallows, unsure as a mayfly
  when to rise,
or where the shoreline runs, or how I'll ever catch the breeze
  to get there.

7.17.2017

Now that I'm getting older,
   summers aren't so long,
they flash, burn, vanish,
   and I can't keep them straight,
though last night under Sirius,
   I got the feeling that somehow
I'd beaten my undoing
   and the grand show of starlight
rained down for me, a spectacle worth seeing,
   the way it hard-landed on my deck
and splattered silver everywhere,
   though maybe a bit showy in that galaxy kind of way,
since now I'm getting older
   and take my nuances—thistle, pod, seed—like a child again,
wide-eyed, slowed-down, and day-by-day.

10.31.2017

It's said the great bass player Jaco Pastorious
once heard symphonies in the yellow trees.

It's so hard to play this, he thought,
exactly as I heard it.

The sky's dialect, the manic wind,
the low notes of rain.

How they slide down the windowpane,
how you thrummed the fretless neck.

How once you held in your hands
exactly what you heard in the sky,

a grace-note no one survives.
A costly way of asking, *I wonder why.*

A HERON IN THE WORKS

Beside those things I've done and those left undone,
lay down the fact that every morning I woke up in ignorance,
even when the light fell across my face, but arose as best I could,

a twitch here, a dread there, and with the tools
I'd gathered along the way, set out to patch the sky,
renew a vow, shimmer in my boots, and find the book

of teachings the old masters, broadcasting from their caves,
said centuries ago would open up wherever I am,
whenever I see just right the broken things

that lay like driftwood in my fallen yard:
the gray, dew-lit feather on the woodpile,
husk of cicada, the chilling downdraft, the soft rot

of things I love and hold until I know in my bones
that even though what I have isn't satisfactory,
what I have is enough. Besides, I've got this ache

to search out and dream stuff
that isn't stuff at all: a tree and its spirit,
a sky and its face, a river and its wish

to leave its wisdom at my feet where I stand
in the current, pulled and directed, come
and gone, a heron in the works, with leaving on its mind.

THE TRUE SUBJECT:
SELF-PORTRAIT WITH DOGWOODS

The true subject of poetry is the loss of the beloved.
Dropping their tiny crosses,
    the dogwoods know it,
        and I've come to see

what they mean, and what they mean is this:
a sentence fires up,
    and already its ending looms
        somewhere down the line.

Begin one, as I do now, and watch its cavalcade,
as it swerves away from the ruin
    of your neighborhood, skirts
        the gaping schoolyard where love

first went bad, then comes to rest, mothlike, by the candle
you lit in the church you've not visited
    in years. See? Structure and choice
        go hand-in-hand, one thing taken,

one left behind—the ghost in every sentence is the ghost
of loss, nothing could have been other
    than it was, but still the implication
        that more is there for the taking,

a blossom-fall within the sentence that cannot contain it:
this is what the dogwoods mean when they tell us
    the loss of the beloved
        is the true subject of poetry.

HEART ROOM

In memoriam, Mary Oliver

I read somewhere in a poem by Mary Oliver
     that we need more room in the heart for love,
that we need to be like those birds that dart and swoop
     because they have little to weigh them down,
which amounts to an act of vision,
     a way to clean the lens
we bring to the world when we need to see the world
     as it is, without fear of growing old,
without haste to heal the hurt we've left
     in our wake . . . just a reliable way
of helping each other amble along between the blues
     of our coming and going.
                    Heart room, then, a place,
for trees and birds and the love of those who can fly away
     without a sigh for you or me because they love the clear blue sky
where, since I was a boy, I have so much wanted to be.

II

WHAT LIGHT HE SAW
I CANNOT SAY

Big sun already, fourth of July; waves
of heat creasing vision; magnolia
scent strong-arms the yard;
exhausted zinnias buckle under.

Huge morning wanders my way,
familiar, supple; I know its swathe
and waste, its storm-cowl
hung on the horizon.

Some memories you wear like a locket:
my father's last bottle
of Century Club half-empty,
stowed away deep in his dark closet

beside the green suede shoes
he bought in New York City
and wore only on special occasions.
He'd dance, laugh, and swig, swig

laugh, and dance again.
I found that bottle
after he died, and those shoes too,
and as it was Independence Day,

and I was a young man
feeling that sole independence
that comes of a father's dying slowly
and fading away,

I put them on, and drank
from that bottle and twirled,

and for the moment, lost myself
in his stride and left nothing

to the imagination: now the world
blurred for me, as it must have for him,
alone with his promise
that he'd never pass a night

in the home where I'd placed him.
True to his word, he did not see
the light of the following day.
What light he saw I cannot say.

But I keep that bottle on my desk.
And sometimes I dance with my daughter
and give her stories about the man,
spinning hand-in-hand,

deep in his rhythm,
again and again only
because I know too well
how this dance will end,

how she must learn for herself
how heartless love's home
can be, how love too is a lodestone,
and how hard it pulls us to it.

WHATEVER'S LEFT OF AMERICA, I CLAIM IT: FOURTH OF JULY

Seasons pursuing each other, the indescribable crowd is gathered, it is the
Fourth of July, what salutes of cannons and small arms!
—WALT WHITMAN, "Song of Myself"

Whatever's left of America, I
claim it here and now, not as mine, but ours,
to chart and parse the nouns and verbs that work
overtime to get it right, the job well done:
our hands, palms-down on the drafting tables,
the transoms above the workroom doors, wide
open to the drafts that rise from the streets—
poems now for the days when some say poems are passé.

Tinseled stars and July bunting hang
from porticos, fires crackle overhead,
as the noon's blaze drives us indoors
until the blue night-sky calls us back
to the flash and pop of stars and guns
and all the new words for all the new days.

JACKSON SQUARE

From the high balcony where dawn falls
through fret-works of tulip tree and live oak
and lands in soot colors, and a magnolia
garlands the street-life thrumming below . . .
from that balcony, above iron-worked flowers, above
it all, you seem to float, and were this a boy's dream,
I'd stop here, castaway, hoping the moon's last silver
would wash me down good enough to make me new
in your eyes just before sunrise, and bring you down here.

No boy now, but full still of dreaming, I
have landed here to see you again and call up what that boy
saw in the sky when he was so full of himself
he rattled and rolled through the gorgeous world,
and felt the magnolia, tulip, and oak
shimmer through him like love . . . but only *like love*, he said,
not love itself, until an ache born years ago within him
returns through the gaunt years,
stirring his tongue in this moonlit place, under you now,

to say, *I know that boy, and now I see*
he never went away. I came here, the trees once bent
over me as they are now, brooding, and I fought them back,
as now, under the faceless stars riding the dark
water—it courses through our lives who live and die
on its shore. Can you hear the river that carries
those stars downstream? It carries so much more
as it goes, all things that blossom, all glances given
to moments bright and shallow, minnow-quick

in the mind, and sun motes too that angle sharply
and die downward in its depth, all these things go,
and so no longer a boy I thought I'd come and tell
you how all the time that's left is left now

here to us, where a balcony stands for complexity
and distance, and my street-life for a common devotion.
Wings I would dream were I the boy I once was.
Being a woman, you turn and go through ghosting curtains.
The river's green odor, and a storming ozone ride hard

downwind. My gut's a clinched fist. What to say? I need
a simile to get out of here. None come. So say what I mean:
lawless crowds revel home now, tattered and frayed, dawn
spirits steam upward through manholes, grackles shuffle their wings,
drop from those trees that once loomed over my passion,
waddle across the way, and cry their parched cackle.
A dry morning settles on Jackson Square, and then here
you are, down now, you've come for the day, your hand finds mine,
draws it toward silks that fall from your shoulder, like dew.

THE DEAD AND DYING

All this talk about the dead and dying, when will it stop?
Let's agree for now they've left us here,
      deserters who walked away to places we do not know,
and let's also remember that Whitman said
      these deserters are more numerous than we'd thought.

I don't do inventories anymore (they are too depressing),
but stack the number of dead
      beside the number left here still wondering what's next,
and I see an evening fat
      with morning glories, up-reaching, in early dew,

but with noon so hung on the coming horizon
we miss the moment's flash and bloom.
      O it's hot but it's a dry heat we say,
and so yes, we can take it, though the blooms will stand down
      and return tomorrow . . .

we say that too, quietly to ourselves, and half-believe it
because it gets us up in the morning
      when what we dreamed comes true,
and there are flowers on the trellis again,
      in that pure and passing shade of heavenly blue.

DRINKING NETTLE TEA,
READING MILAREPA

Mid-spring, lime-toned palette, nothing odd there,
>   but here in my lap *The Hundred Thousand Songs of Milarepa,*
the Tibetan yogi, plenty odd, and hard-grown in Himalayan bedrock
whose songs find me now, high lonely and half-happy in my
>   Ozark station-study.

Think tendrils, how they lace their way through centuries, hit the
>   heart's trellis,
>   and coil there with the long song the yogi sang
about home, how it's like a rasp filing away one's body, word, and mind.
It's time, Milarepa, I say this: home now, where I belong, has got me
>   warped and woofed,

fit to be tied down, a nesting man, and good at it,
>   except when those blue gales blow, the ones
you sat through, and asked: *Why not then prepare a boat for the*
>   *crossing?*
I confess now I have no such boat, though in outright green abundance

I have these many, splendid things, though I know now that they too
>   have me:
>   a reading chair I'd kill to keep, books to die for, and
>   one carpet,
or several, really, I want under my feet at all times, and miss them when
>   they're not.
And noodles—O noodles!—hot, spiced, and loved as noodles have never
>   been loved . . .

But, I have listened to you, Milarepa, cave-bound, spliced through the
>   gaps of my living,
>   come down to say, and I quote, *how using the mind to*
>   *watch the mind,*

I am happy, that the reward is to die without regret,
that practicing meditation in solitude is, in itself, a service to the people.

Consider me then, Milarepa, well served and grateful. I am watching myself.
     And I say,
          if my regrets were leaves on maples,
I could make a maple-forest, but instead, will settle in and watch spring's
          easy rising.
I want to make a tea of all this, reduce it, never lose it.

Once you see this gentle rising, words fail us, you said, from every cave,
               mountain pass, every scree and angle you worked
in the killing light of the high winters—a bleach to my vanity.
The body is but a magic spell, made of mist and fog. You said that too.
     So I say, here I come,

mist and fog, fog and mist. Holy rolling thunder, I drift, travel
               toward those I hold dear under soft yellow skies,
not quite hand-in-hand, but of common purpose, at least, alive enough
to know the difference between the truth of love and the pack of lies

that hound us half our life, until one day, with any luck at all,
               we sit bolt upright and see an ordinary thing set sail
(from a corner of the bedroom, maybe, sun-struck, a dust-mote),
and it's bright and moving toward us, and we say *I will start here, and*
          I will not fail.

SUMMER SOLSTICE

1.

Another summer solstice sauntered by last night with a strawberry
  moon in tow,
   then passed on to make room
for the vastness with no name I can say, no address I can find,
    which is the way of solstices and moons,
to come, dim down, vanish, and leave us that dull bone-ache we call
  pilgrim.

2.

If wishes were trees, the trees would be falling . . .
  I heard that once in a silly song, and yet, sad as I am because
  I have so few wishes now,
our old hickory is still bent by noon's druggy heat, but otherwise
    stands sentry to every passing dream I've had about
  escape and light
and seeing things as they are, only once, just once, with abandon
  and joy.

3.

I have thought highly of trees most of my life, how they go nowhere,
  drilled down in their place,
and yet open up everywhere to everything
    that drops and settles in their sky-scoring limbs.
But lately, I confess I'm unsettled by the dreams snagged in my hickory,

how every morning, another one, webbed through its branches, spangled
  with dew,
  attractive, of course, until the sun comes, hauling memories
of the great teachers I've read at one time or another
    who said things like *stay in a place where you will*
  be happy,
and *if you fear being scattered, fence yourself in,*

to which I'd add only, *rest easy in the kindnesses that have gathered*
        around you
        because they are many, and so I have hunkered down
        among them,
I have decided to leave alone the busyness of the traveler,
            to stand down and hear what comes through the trees
and to see what rises in my heart, shaded and unexposed.

4.

It is, after all, high time I understood the world,
        the one I know is broken, always in motion,
and teaches through its brokenness, through its shards
            and hulls scattered at my feet,
even in the grandest palaces and coolest cafés and greenest fairways,

they're steaming away, even there, even here, teachings,
        more than I can count, and always shifting, falling,
more than I can know in that instant of my life
            when maybe I wake and see what's happening
as it happens, as it holds in balance, for an instant only,
        the broken wave of the coming day.

POEM FOR HIGH SUMMER

1.

What I want to say daily diminishes,
falls off, runs down,
                    heads toward the dry season, deep July,
where light hangs around for so long,
and the will to speak lams it, leaving
behind the scratch-notes of cicadas,
                              the sense they bring
that whatever vacuum nature is said to abhor,
words abhor it more.

And so here I am, nearly speechless,

and the summer ultimatum to leave well enough alone,
to listen and bend nothing to the sentence,
makes more sense than ever.

I have, in fact, great hope for my coming silence
because the plan is fundamental, seasonal:

fall silent and hear
                    the worn-down world deep in the dry grass
and know that nothing scuds into view
                          that needs more than I can give it,
that whatever's clamoring for attention
                          takes nothing less than I have.

2.

After the summer solstice,
                    the steady decline of light.
After the steady decline of light,
                          a little of this, a little of that,

but nothing of moment, until the hickory in the yard, shorn of
        its glory
by the ordinary things that come and take us all, like ice and wind
        and weariness,
shudders and buds,
                        and very slightly greens,
and presses through the longer evenings that now grow even longer.

May I call this a life?

May I sit and watch the blazing cycle of colors and codes,
amazed by my amazement,
                        ciphering just so the wind-rattle,
        the down-draft,
a little different this year than last,
                        and still say to myself I've done
        all I could
to see what was here from every angle, every line, every latitude?
Have I seen my father, dead and gone these forty years, in every
        shade and hue?

3.

When all seems lost, inventory what's left:
those mornings our deck became the splashdown landing-zone for
        the sun's light-river,
the patterned shadows that spilled from the lattice-work
        across the garden,
the narcotic tick and hiss of his sprinkler . . .
                        there's my father standing on his porch,
his first cigarette in hand as the day gets under way, and his yard greens . . .

All these obsidian moments, hard, hard to see, and never going
        anywhere.

What in this world, O Lord, do *they* mean?

This happens only because that happened?

                                    A way at least to understand

how we might live in the present moment,

indecipherable, inscrutable,

                         as if the past *really* happened (it did),

and never left us (it didn't).

It's all so simple: a broken world long ago, yes,

but broken down in bundles that return, teach, assure, comfort, love,

       and show

the way forward,

                  like that old stone-carving from Mohenjo Daro, 4,500

       years ago,

where the man sits in a lotus position,

                        hands on knees,

and wonders, as I do, as did my father, when he'll get the peace and

       quiet to hear

what his living has to say, song-note

by song-note, shard by shard.

He could just as well be my father, that man from Mohenjo Daro,

the greensward rolled out before him,

suburban logic, though, and having long forgotten

       that *beauty's in the looking for it,*

my father stubs out his cigarette,

worries about the dry season coming, turns,

and strides away through a silky swirl of smoke.

SIX THINGS I KEEP IN MIND
AS THE END OF THE WORLD APPROACHES
AND I AM TALKING TO MYSELF

1.

Those ancient, gilded days you tote in your head, but not so ancient
      you can't remember them
when you're feeling low, as the End of the World Approaches . . .
      they're a prison.

2.

The way you remodel the wreckage you left behind, which in time
      engulfs you
even before the End of the World Approaches . . .
      it's a hair-shirt, take it off.

3.

Those arguments for the beautiful you figured others missed, the ones
      with salvia and foxglove,
and a villa, and a piazza, while the End of the World Approaches . . .
      that's a vanity.

4.

All those solos you hold dear to your heart: Hendrix, a sunrise,
      the single cry of the single bird
in the dead of night, as the End of the World Approaches . . . *they*
      don't care about you.

5.

The passage from Whitman where he says there'll never be any more
      perfection than now, nor
any more heaven or hell, and still the End of the World Approaches . . .
      you weren't listening.

6.

Our brief and temperate lives, with ferns, in which you never saw
      brevity and temperance as virtues,
as the End of the World Approaches . . . *there's time, still time,*
      to rethink all this.

DEAD RECKONING

I've been dead-reckoning all my life,
                         and never knew it.

How far have I come? Where did I go?

Those were the questions I considered.

Not, *What is that purple radiance when I close my eyes?*
Which never concerned me,
nor the constellations Ferris-wheeling across the sky . . .
I didn't care.

Confession: I should've looked around more,
certain now that nothing is useless,
even the leaf-stained sky,
                         or the half-tones of green light
that fall through the jack pine,
                         and the Kirtland's warbler that lives there,
and would perish anywhere else under the sun.

That's a way of going I've come to know late in life . . .
    Step, see, step, see,
and know for everything kicked up on the path,
    ten thousand things flicker by unseen,

yet counterpoint their way into our lives
as something felt we don't quite trust, but feel all the same,
eddying, pulling us, holding our hands and keeping us arm in arm,
known but unknown,
the dark pull of a universe calling us home.

AMERICAN CITY,
BROKEN BODY

I'd like to tell you one of those lanky stories
that begins with a great aunt, white-haired,
dressed in the old way that signals privilege,
the crystal-blue eyes slightly downturned
that say *my house holds secrets*
a little boy might leave well enough alone.

Specifics? In a lanky story, there's plenty of room:
Victorian, camphor, a collage of habits and ideas
that won't fold under the weight of the years
that conceived them, gave them life, and raised them up—
stanchions and planks and cells I still feel deep inside me,
though I've spent a life breaking them as best I could.

What matters now is a country that renders a body
breakable, and leaves those bodies justified
in the breaking by an inscrutable energy,
a habit energy the Buddhists call it from cool mountains
where habits can kill a saint, though not
so quickly as down here on the mean streets

of American cities. I think of escape
velocity, I want to know the speed
a body needs to get out, to render down the violence
with love, to breathe and drink and eat without fear.
I have no figures for the math of human suffering.
The book that ciphers in this manner

is a travel book to me and tells
of a place far away from the place
where I came to believe in things
that don't exist—the beautiful, say,
mixed with lightning and always horizons
and always more intense than stars.

TO SING IT ANOTHER WAY

I'll play it and tell you what it is later.

—MILES DAVIS, on "If I Were a Bell"

He'd play it first, so he said, and tell us what it was later.
     I'm in the drive-thru at the coffee shop
thinking about that when a house finch with a slash of scarlet
     hung above its beak popped out of the hedge
under the cashier's window and gave me a look
     that only a finch can give, as if to say,
What in God's name are you doing here, lost man?
     Then flitted away into air and vastness and mystery and doubt.
And so began my unknowing, my gut that I'd never tell a soul
     what it was like to look deeply into a finch's eye,
crystal, future-telling clear, but full of judgment,
     full of knowing deep in its heart (then deep in mine too)
that we'd arced across the hedge,
     headed nowhere under these darkened skies, but daily believing
if we sang it just right, the world might turn out otherwise.

III

NOCTURNE:
DRINKING SONG

First-quarter moon, August
running down; star-stippled sky
over earth's battled keel.
Bourbon jive in moth light.

We've done this before
and raised our glasses to those
who've done this before,
who've stayed the course

and left us behind. Godspeed.
The moon's got no use for us now.
Wind congregates, shoves off.
Leaf-shudder. Hold on. We're coming.

BULLION

I have so much to tell you
        about slatch and lapse,
the lull of brown, fall's breakdown, drop-leaf dance,
about the high-tension sizzle-note that crickets fiddle and die for,
and the fadeout of an Arkansas dusk
        when ashen swallows loop and roll
and their diminished cries seem the cries of some outriding soul.

I have so much to tell you
        about the last marvel I saw:
I was on one of the old blacktops that heads out of town,
late sunlight prismed through the heat's haze, hay bales
bleared to gold . . . What could I tell you now
        that would not be true?
Exile, hostage, prisoner, lover, monarch, that's what I was,

in a pasture rendered down to the eye's bullion,
        and for the moment, that was enough,
but then gauze-winged mayflies, and lift-off from a ribbon
of water, the merest miracle of water, and what was moving
was moving upward, our god-born afterlife pantomimed
        in a pasture in the middle of nowhere
off an old blacktop I'd taken in hopes of outrunning
dross and ballast, the twin spirits of our coming dissolution;
        so what I have to tell you now
is that just before we come apart, we arc away
from one another, mayflies I say, blinded by the sun's confetti,
and that once, I had wished you and I were here together,
        afterglow and corona, ascending
from the miracle, and king and queen now of our long,
        blooming blacktop.

HOW WE LEAVE THE WORLD

Enter stage-left, pirouette, take a bow or not, exit stage right. Gone.
    Poor Yorick. Still and all, I want to say what I've seen,
how loneliness lives side by side with luminosity,
how the trellis louvers the sun so that it falls at my feet in green slats
and how, after the day's garish display runs its course, and night
    drapes its gray wool everywhere,
still, there's solitude under this star-glitter, and no one's dancing.

So here's the Hell of it—trellis, sunlight, beauty's carnage,
    I live in the spectacle, behind the leaves,
light-pierced, enthralled, and know I can't love this carnage enough,
and that's what puddles the spirit that clouds the eye.
Still, boll and pod swell, fester, and break, seeds float, fall, dig in . . .
    late summer nails it every year,
and transfigures the yard: the milkweed's cracked, the maple's burning,

we crack and burn as well, but not like this, we're not that good
    at making do with what we've got
because we cannot say where love's obsession will take us next.
Meanwhile, autumn's quartered in the cool spell. Soon, it will fire
the tips of every leaf, it will break out and leave me
    here alone, as the season cruises by
on translucent wings, and the earth's Amen rises up in a dark flock.

SONG IN LATE SUMMER FOR SAPPHO, HERACLITUS, AND LED ZEPPELIN

1.

All afternoon at the wide, high window, summer settling hard now
    across the land,
    small deaths rattle away in the dry snap of the season,
    and I wish this window were the window of the world's soul.
And suddenly, so it is.

2.

The starling scores a scimitar path across the sky,
    then vanishes into the blue of the magnolia shade;
    spokes of sunlight shred the tree tops just before dusk
    when dusk cloaks us, and we know an impeccable regret we
    cannot shake.
    And so we walk in the world, strong-shouldered.

Now, and here, what's envisioned has every chance of coming true . . .

3. Sappho

Summer's sky, a millrace of clouds, browbeats the ridgeline.
    Rainfall sizzles down over the Ozarks,
    its hiss and pop on leaf and flower is the ear's Braille.
    I cannot otherwise imagine a possible life, another downpour,
    a finer sound.
    July 24th, and tonight's moon is nearly full, waxing toward
    Sappho and her wide-eyed illumination.

4.

This seen world, it outshines us at every turn, it dims us down,
    and we must flicker, if we flicker at all,
    in the light of our own making.

Now, and here, what's envisioned has every chance of coming true . . .

5.

Furthermore, the elm shakes its light from quivering leaves,
       showing how brightness slips away from us
       even as brightness remains the herald of our days.
       In the surge-flash of morning, in the soft finish of afternoon,
       both splendid in their order and column, yet still the violet doubt
       like a small bruise grows within, and the view
       from my window unravels
       ever so slightly.

6. Heraclitus and Led Zeppelin

Heraclitus got it right: you don't step twice into the same river.
       And you don't look twice into the same soul, I'd add.

But Led Zeppelin got it right too: the song remains the same.
       Tatter, tatter, shred, fray, dissolve, and fade away.

7.

So the canvas, over-stretched a bit, has come undone at the corners,
       and I am here at this window gathering evidence for my ending:
       starlings arc up and out of the frame, and will not return,
       the oaks are entering the incumbent stillness of duskfall.

Day's diffusing now, its long haul downward
       leaves much to the imagination.
       O merciful God, they used to say.

Nowadays?
       Crank it up, we say: fireflies rise, moon-showers fall,
       and the night-blooming flowers are pearls in the garden.
       With our darkened hearts,
       we sit here in the sheen, and cruise through it all.

Nowadays?
       Crank it up, we say, *O merciful God,*
       we've loved what we've seen.

FIVE THINGS I SAID
TO THE GREAT BLUE SUMMER SKY

After hearing Eddie Vedder and Neil Finn's version of
"Throw Your Arms Around Me" by Hunters & Collectors

1.

Dead-notes of dry leaves sing out from the hickory limbs,
waiting, so they can fall and rise, like me, into the great blue
      summer sky.

2.

Doves drop from the hickory to the seeds heaped below the feeder,
the bounty of this world under the great blue summer sky.

3.

Anyway, I'm sound-tracking Steve Earle's "Transcendental Blues"
      in a mash-up
with the neighborhood hawk, and under this great blue summer sky,

4.

I don't know what else to do *in the darkest hour of the longest night,*
except to wait, as always, for the the great blue summer sky,

5.

feeling as I do that it will come my way, and you'll throw your arms
      around me,
and we'll sleep and die under the great blue summer sky.

MEDITATION ON A STATEMENT
BY PASCAL

Dusk's all over the place;
                            the sun's a blood-spot through the black locust,
the locust is spattered with grackles.
My yard's a Jackson Pollack.

The family's gathered together to small-talk the evening
                                      down to its sable end.
Above us, tongueless stars burn in the pinwheeling sky.
God's a turnstile, letting us through, one by one. Click, click.

Tyranny is wanting to have by one means
                              what can only be had by another.

The figured world's my tyrant.
Heliotropic horizon, a rack of clouds on the move,
an arrangement of birds . . .
It's such a fine and fat scene,
but what it gives up to us is gaunt and hard:
                                    I mean,
crickets scrape it out on their fiddle-legs,
then fall silent.

But when we're done talking tonight, we too fall into silence, gaunt
        and hard.

Meanwhile and anyway, the locust conspires, and sends its shadow
        across the yard.

FIELD PRAYER

A very long time ago (as these stories begin),
where the wagon-road stopped dead by a long field of cotton,
Willie Foster, who came down on this earth
to play his harp for Muddy Waters,
told me, *If you hit the wrong note, hold it 'til it sounds right.*
Not much good at harp music,
I believe in tangling with whatever's gone wrong
until the air around me clears,
and there's peace or exhaustion or both.

Willie died a while ago,
but sometimes now when the heat's warped the tree-line
into wave-patterns,
I hear that wrong note,
the shimmer-note of human suffering,
and all I can say is, *help me find a way to hold it until I perish,*
or the shimmering stops.

Either way, I'll have done what I could, and shimmered, and gone.

SHANK OF THE AFTERNOON:
AN INVITATION

Shank of the afternoon,
      August walking tall now
through the backyard,
      leaf-littered and brown.

Down by the river,
      the world's no better. The air
doesn't move. Or can't.
      Maybe won't. It's all in E Minor

anyway, the sad, restless key,
      I mean, so death is banked
under the still whips
      of the green willow down

in that E Minor air.
      You get this, I know you do,
we're born to it,
      so take my hand. Let's go there.

THE SOUND OF WATER

Half my life, I've had this river in mind I cannot get down
in words, although once on the banks of the Tennessee
      I thought I heard how it might be done,
          I figured I'd found the score . . .

You wait a lifetime for these things, I know,
and when they come, baggy and slip-covered
      by obsession, you can't believe they'll
          deliver what they promise, but that day,

brown water the color of an old sadness
sludged through the heart of Knoxville,
      and I remember it as if it were yesterday,
          every dimple and swirl on the river's back

slowly resolving into blankness, a river
spreading its rumors of the featureless end
      that stares us in the face, telling its god-awful tales
          of the headlong downhill that shuttles us there.

It wasn't hard to see the river's schematic: swallows
dropped in over the willow bank, lightly touched down
      on the water, and were gone, and there was glory
          on their wings as faith and doubt vaulted

upward into an absolute blue and perished. *Good riddance,*
I remember thinking. So why huddle within ourselves
      like spiked pods? Open instead and ask: *Why fear*
      the warp-speed
          of a season's progress? The willows loll now

in their penitent stations by the river. All movement—
a thought's vector, my heart's chamber, a sparrow's fall—
     aims at contrition. Sorrow has emptied out the thistle,
       compassion taken the river out of town,
   around the bend,

and left us here on the banks of the Tennessee, our faith
a starched collar, oblivion the sound of water
     that would not stop for us, that would always pass us by,
       and the sound of water now the only sound
   in the world.

UP AGAINST THE STEEL-GRAY SKY

Up against steel-gray sky, the plane that has you
arcs overhead, tips its wing, and comes
down where I wait, in terminal light, splendid
in anticipation. Nothing can hold us
to old promises now, now that the old ways
clang and clatter in the soul's dungeon.
Your face renovates,
and we're gossamer for the moment
I hold you, late afternoon spilling down
around us. Blank-faced travelers shuffle by.
History's figured in a glance though,
and in a glance I see you as I'd have you
see yourself: calm in this wide wind that brought you
to me, quiet now as the coming night, and as lovely.

RIVER STONE, WITH SIMONE WEIL

I love to stand to the leeward side of the light,
                behind the trellis gaudy with morning glory,
watch the sun wester away and imagine the day I'll do the same.
It's like stalking myself from behind, but I can't
manage the point of departure, the moment I lose stanchion and stave
and relax into rigidity—it's all so opal, the light
                lustering mysteries I've spent a life
      wondering about.

I could not have wished to be alive at a better time than this,
                when all has been lost, Simone Weil said.
In desperation, there's room to move, in need, there's abundance.
I've decanted my sadness into a flagon, and thrown it over
       my shoulder.
A river stone, upright in the down-rush, could not be more cocksure
       of its place than I.
To the leeward side of light, I am always standing, poised.
      Late swallows yaw yaw into the dark abundance.

IT HAS BEEN SAID THE WORLD
CANNOT BE NAMED:
A LOVE SONG

It has been said the world cannot be named,
that naming is a prison, that what passes so quickly before us—
the up-curl of light in a girl's eye, the rasp of late-afternoon cicadas—
rolls steady into view, and just as quickly deserts
the very place we last saw them: the far corner of the neighbor's yard
just before sundown under the maple's yellow purging light.

The very same light, by the way, that leaves us
a little pale and washed out, and unprepared for more words.
Not ready for another intervention.
Not down with more interruption.

All is quiet now,
and only this will do: a moment of coming undone with you, right here,
      right now,
as autumn passes through us again, and we feel nothing
need be said about the hum of what's humming,
the drone of what's droning,
the long bend of the long coming night.

THE BETTER MISTAKE

You've been making the wrong mistakes.
—THELONIOUS MONK

As we all have.
I can no more unhear the music
I've heard
than unread the books
I've read,
un-see the failing light
I've seen fall and splinter
across the faces
I've loved that vanished
overnight
and left nothing in their wake.
So I confess now,
below a stunner of a pink sky
and Monk streaming
across the yard
that I have made the wrong mistakes.
Fallen down for words.
Crashed for notes. Spoken
when silence held the room,
left justice for dead, my father
half-alive in his bed
who returns now to remind me
that when I saw him last
he turned away as I declared
I loved him.
I cannot un-turn that turning away.
So I have clarity.
The clarity of hurt. Of scar. Of direction.
One note at a time, then,
building the scales that move forward

scaffolded on hope,
the better mistake that Monk made,
and the one that leaves me here, blessed
and flawed by the pink and fade of another day.

IV

NOCTURNE: PASCAL SAYS

I think it's too full, this moon:
snow-light careens off the snowfield,
blinding us to all
that half-lit yearning deep inside

to live, to breathe, and finally to see
how much we have left to do before we go.
But Pascal says it's not good to have everything
one needs, unwise to be too free.

And it's true, December's a shakedown cruise:
leaf-rot simmers under my window,
the air's anorexic, lamp and book
are a burden, and I conclude I am

too free, that I have all I need.
Close the book, kill the lamp.
The moon's full, but Pascal says it's loss I want.
So I shut my eyes. And read.

MORNING'S GLORY

I woke up this morning
obsessed with the latticed light
laid in slats across the floor—
    a ladder leading nowhere.

Later, morning's glory
gone downhill while high
overhead, the dead glare
    of noon vultures homing in.

Our home, yours and mine,
    here in the offing,
here in the place of dreaming
    and hearts that climb and soar

and sink and fall, and always
    on good days, the days
we pray for, the ones that come
    once, and come no more.

TO A FRIEND WHO
WOULD TELL STORIES

High noon. A storm crawls by, and it's late to be
still in bed, but I am for once high lonesome
in a motel where lives have come undone
on these wine-dark beds big as wine-dark seas;
to this sea, though, I've taken the Shakespeare
she gave me with her young hands and the Berryman
on Shakespeare, an old hand now up and gone,
and I'd give her what he once gave to me:

Hear the winds brawl? Listen. They brawl for you.
Think of Ulysses. And the soughing sound
of his sea. Now you're there, and there is art,
a long run of riper days under blue
skies—I read this in your eyes, and wrote it down.
Take it. Please. For anything less have no heart.

WHEN SAINTS AGREE

I've never met a saint,
but if I ever do, I've got a question ready to go:
That tulip tree over there in full bloom, I'll ask,
how does it look to you?
Little short of perfect? Maybe a distraction?
Maybe just a bloom on just a tree on just an ordinary afternoon?
I bet all the saints would agree though:
what took them by the spirit

                         and shook them down,

light-raked and dawn-dropped,
what most made them the folks they came to be,
cannot be said in the very words
our very spirits called upon to do the job:

Holy,
    Sacred,
        Divine,
            Celestial,

no, no,
none of these will do, which leaves the rest of us deep in our garrisons,
dug-in, unmoving,
unsaintly, without a clue, listening for the signal in the noise:

a wing-whistle,
                cricket-scratch,
winds that hiss through the longleaf pines,
anything that transcends itself but leaves these traces behind.

That would be enough: the seed-sound in the seed,
the oak-note in the acorn,
                  the blue-scale in the black sky.

But here from where I stand on this earth,
believing in jubilation,
and listening hard as I can,
I still cannot say why
or even wonder when
it all began.

OLD SONG FOR
MY YOUNG DAUGHTER

My daughter's reached the age when she asks me questions
about my past as if she were a colonial explorer, intent
on acquisition, but not on understanding the old place,

the ups and downs of campus revolt, the Hare Krishna
ochre robes, the life of the mind The Beatles brought back,
the early flattening of the great arcs: Kennedy, King, Jimi, Janice.

She can't get past the bell-bottoms and maybe rightly so.
Pinned and wriggling in the jaundiced light of a Polaroid,
I am to her an exhibition of the way things used to be,

and not a great exhibition, exactly, not the kind the critics say
you have to see, but one they'd mark as a curiosity,
a Fabergé egg, maybe, you'd visit one of those afternoons

you got lit up by a double cappuccino and found yourself
in a big city with a small museum, well curated—
another phrase these critics use—and full of things like me:

an ornamental, good egg, curious, even essential
in that alluring kind of odd way,
whose purpose, when all is said and done, is a mystery

and whose mystery is what keeps you standing there,
searching out the reason for all the useless detail,
the meaningless gesture of a jewel, or maybe just reading

a generation's last will and testament: a tie-dyed affair that states
without reservation and with the pure joy I'd wish for her,
we're still so grateful we're still not dead.

NOTES TOWARD A
PRESENT LIFE

2:30 a.m., southwestern sky, waxing moon.
So big, I'll push my luck, and call it full.

⚭

I'm so lonely, I say.
Two weeks ago, there were cardinals, and I wasn't lonely at all.
The sky was gray, and the birds were red.
Red-birds, my father called them, and they were his favorite.

⚭

He was a joyous and troubled man
because we are a joyous and troubled people.
So I bring my father's birds now to my loneliness.

⚭

To live a good life, an old monk once told me, first learn to breathe.
Then, and only then, look and listen.
So, forget the dusty red-birds, I say now.
My loneliness is getting along very well without them.

⚭

What happens in the heart of loneliness is a wind,
a slow lift in the air that ferries away
the last leaf on the mulberry tree.
Loneliness is like that.

⚭

Somewhere in the *Dhammapada,*
there's a passage that goes,
only recite a precious few teachings
but dump the passion, anger, and ignorance,
and the skies will clear for you.

As it turns out, I only know a few teachings,
and they are wrapped up in leaf-fall,
and how the sun spatters everything
it crosses with burning light.
But always, a crossing, always a fire.

A prayer then: *may there always be*
in all I see
this crossing, and an indicated shore, with light,
and a way to get there, with joy,
and only this,
and nothing more.

DEEP BLUES

Try it when you get a chance,
and the wind drops
that furrowed face
across the Mississippi,
wrinkled with star-
light reflecting back
at you askance

enough to make you wonder
why you ever came this way:
head down Highway One,
east of the levee and
stop smack-dab in Rosedale,
then head south to Leland
to catch it,

a white boy's plunder
and refuge: I did that
once and learned
that if you pull
from your pocket
your very own harmonica
anywhere between Gunnison

and Greenville and an ancient man
says to you, *I used to play*
a little mouth harp a long time ago,
you're about to hear
a thing you've never heard before,
and you'll recall it as a storm,
or thunder, but that won't do

because what really happened
was his slow pull on your B-flat

was a hard wail you never knew,
and will never know, so you decided,
when you got your harp back,
you'd just put it
in your pocket, and leave,

and pray for safe passage
back to the land of the living
and dying that you know,
over the levee,
over the furrowed face on the river,
to the place you came from,
and now must go.

SLAG WATCH

I'm not so watchful anymore as the years slag down
    in great heaps of wasted looking.
My eyes grow dull, I'm deaf to songs
    I once sang out loud, with joy.

Is something there? I ask. *No? Nothing?* I don't know,
    but this, yes, I still see this: streamers gather
and skate across my eyes, autumn collects itself,
    falls, and leaves

nothing much to say except what I've said in so many versions
    the world has taken to turning
its back on me when I speak: look now, a hawk in flight,
    a spark from its wing

arcs down to a bone-dry field, and for an instant,
    a flash of maybe fire or inspiration,
but anyway, gratitude for being here at this moment
    without desire,

when once I saw the holy fire of the burning world:
    an autumn palette
restores the ancient wisdom,
    and again, gratitude is in the air.
The nature of mind is clear light; these old stains only accidents.
    Edgy, clean October, stilled in anticipation,
hones its chill. I know what autumn means.
    Age requires a new liturgy:

I have seen all those things I once believed fade away for so long,
    I find it hard to trust
all those things I now can see. So I talk to myself:
    you can't utter yourself into life, I say,

as ospreys do in free fall, and there's sadness in thinking you can.
   What then is the human cry?
And why does it come so slowly, ever nearing the end?
     Of course, lines do come to mind—*the great seas sigh*

and moan, we ourselves sigh and moan—and then pass away
   because this is the map of what happens.
But there are so many maps.
    Do I dare draw another?

Here's one: I want to know what moves in the maple
   come every dawn of my daughter's life—
the light-fall just outside her window, may it be yellow and
     gold in its flight and kind and good in its arrival.

For once, clarity lies all around. My yard is in shambles
   of leaf-rot, tree-bark, root, and bulbs.
It all comes and goes so fast I cannot hold it.
    Maybe a prayer would do now,

but for the life of me, I can't remember one quickly enough to say
   what I want said. I have these words,
this chair, this desk, these sun-angled slabs of dark and light,
    shadow and freedom.

Stop. There is nothing else to declare,
   so I hereby declare it:
I have enough, I really do,
    and maybe always have.

TRANSFIGURATION:
GRAY SKY GOOD ENOUGH
TO WEAR

Gray sky cowls overhead.
  It's wool, really, and feels
good enough to wear. True story:
  once when I was a boy

I thought I saw God stride the sky
  just over the sandbox
and hang there long enough
  to slash this memory

deep within me, a moment now
  I'd just as soon lay away
on a shelf and leave it there
  long enough to look up

and see that old world once more,
  without the things I know now
Hell-hounding my trail: that gray sky,
  that wool, and this urge to stand up

and reach so high
  and pull down that cowl
and wear it, and walk down the road,
  and never in my life wonder why.

FOUR THINGS I NEED TO DECLARE, HAVING CAUSED TROUBLE IN MY HOUSE, BEFORE I INHERIT THE WIND

He that troubles his own house, shall inherit the wind.

—PROVERBS 11:9

1.

Let me leave this place, when it's time to go, as clean as I can in that
    Zen kind of way:
        a fire-lit room, rough-hewn floor, white-washed from
        here to there,
a place to sit and wait, a place that barters hope for everything I'll
    soon see.

2.

I'll leave no plan behind, although the oak leaf's down-spiral
    I'd recommend.
        Catch it mid-fall, in the year's mildness, the month done,
        exhausted,
having spent itself in motion: you can rock yourself to sleep now,
    like a wave on the ocean.

3.

The great teacher Patrul Rinpoche once told his students: *go to the*
    hills, forests, and rivers,
        and search for your mind everywhere, in the grass, under rocks,
in the water. And so I did, and left no stone unturned in my search,
    and failed, and was happy.

4.

Summer's aftermath is coming, and I'll sit as always and watch
    its many splendored arrival. Full bloom to dead wither,
    nothing uncovered
stays the same. File it away: comfortable, swayed, rebounding,
    I'm here. Always.

HOMAGE TO THE
KADAMPA MASTERS

They tell me this body of mine I haul
down to the sea, a bare-ribbed skiff
jostling its load, nuzzling chaos,
is my only life-raft to freedom.

So noted. I jostle and nuzzle
and hanker for green waves.
I mostly don't know where I'm going though,
which once bothered me

like an unkindness of ravens
that gathered every morning
and followed me all day long.
But now I'm not bothered at all.

Ravens, thoughts, cares, everything
changes in due time,
and so even the moon,
that same old sky-exiled moon,

runs cold through its phases,
and breaks itself on the hickory—
everything waxes and wanes,
and nothing remains the same.

In my yard, though, broken icons
from the journey: a rudder,
a mizzenmast, a dream
of leaving, a careless care.

IF I BELIEVED IN GODS:
FOR MY STUDENTS

If I believed in gods, in light-shot angles,
      the cloud's bluster and explosion,
I'd raise a cry for the lovely souls I see
      backpacking their griefs and joys down the hallways
and out into the open air,
      blue-roofed, hemispheric,
where griefs have no place, no footing,
      except always they find their place, gain their foothold,
and so my lost souls under the blue sky feel
      the weight on their backs and twitch
and shift their load to make their way a little easier
      until finally one day I hope they'll know
when the time's come to lay it down, as the sun blinks once,
      and drops just out of sight behind the tree-line.
It's then that a dusting of pink will fall through the air.

This should be enough, a gracious plenty,
      as the old folks still say,
to stand here in awe and humility and tell our children
      as clearly as we can what we've seen
and how it felt to see it. And wish them too their own sight-lines,
      their own ways of believing
in more gods than they can count, more songs than they'll sing.
On my best days, I leave it at that, one of the travelers
      on a shore no one else sees,
splendid in his traveling gear, shorn down, light-hearted, and loving
      this world,
      as it unfolds before him with ocean ease.

A POEM IS A BOAT IS THE WORLD
IS MY FATHER

I've studied water in all its forms (rain, river, sleet, snow)
    and words too (chants, curses, songs, prayers),
and always when I do, I see a ship yawed and rolling over rough seas,
    but sailing all the same, course unknown,
except to say at long last it's cruising under the blue star-scape, perfect
    and crystalline,
        the one I've known for years was there. Maybe now that
        I've seen it,
I won't return for days, if I return at all, so happy am I in this wind,
    enthralled by the ancient thrill of making do with the
    right phrases
for all the livelong places I still have never been.

I've studied my father too every day since he died forty years ago.
    He was a gracious and complicated man, and I figure
he always wanted such a life, yawed and distant,
    an island scene maybe from *South Pacific*, a film he loved,
being a WWII man himself, and prone to dance whenever he'd drink
    on the beaches he kept deep inside his heart.

I'd ask him now: *Who doesn't pause, and drink, and celebrate,*
    dreaming of the day that offers up the good breeze and waves,
and words that get it just right? That show us a way to leave here,
    with grace?

Am I wrong to want this? Am I wrong to love the down-rush of sunset
    as if it were a waterfall? An outgoing tide? Am I wrong to wish
you'd not kept your promise and died? To wish you were still here
    beside me?

Once you said we cannot map those places where we live, suffer, and
    fade away.

I ask you now, *who will know them if we don't?*
I've said what I took to be so, and here record the last time I saw you:
     silent as a vault, soon to leave us behind. You were too thin,
didn't care, a falling leaf. Against my better judgment, I left, obsessed
     with only what was there, and so I tell you now, *I too will one day*
     sail on air.

NAGARJUNA'S ELEPHANT

An illusory elephant doesn't exist so it can't go anywhere,
can't stay anywhere, and doesn't come from anywhere.
—paraphrased from Nagarjuna's *Precious Garland*
(2nd–3rd century CE)

Let's clear the air about Nagarjuna's elephant.
About the claim the frost makes as it whitens the grass.
About the promise the dogwood keeps with its crossed bud.
About the geese high overhead on a moonless night.
About my dark heart under a black sky.

The world, according to Nagarjuna, is an elephant
that comes from nowhere so goes nowhere so stays nowhere.
Large, unwieldy, indescribable. Always on the move.

Once I too saw the world-as-elephant.
It happened by slow-falling water in Virginia,
a twilit scene, of course, as these stories go,
with mayflies that rose and flashed
and lasted maybe a second or two and then vanished
into the failing light of a yellow evening.

Nagarjuna and all the sages I know agree:
once you see the coming and going of all things,
what's left is only to feel the great speed
at which these comings and goings
come and go.

So fast, they claim, that old habits of seeing,
big as icebergs, and as cold and heavy, break, fall, and melt away.

It comes and it goes, this elephant and this world, and cannot
be described.

CPSIA information can be obtained
at www.ICGtesting.com
Printed in the USA
LVHW092238150321
681649LV00011B/548

What comes of seeing this, they say, is love.

And so this is what love looks like:
the speed of it all, my daughter's hand in mine, then gone;
the blurring instantly into and out of clarity, the loud crow disappeared
        into the high pine.

The unshaping
of it all.

The unshaping of the whole wide world I've known for years.

Searching for love, I looked closely at Nagarjuna's elephant,
        and that is what I saw.